Teaching Poetry
Book 1

Years 1 & 2

Louis Fidge

Published by Letts Educational
The Chiswick Centre
414 Chiswick High Road
London W4 5TF
Tel: 020 89963333
Fax: 020 87428390
email: mail@lettsed.co.uk
Website: www.letts-education.com

Letts Educational Limited is a division of Granada Learning
Limited, part of the Granada Media Group.

© Louis Fidge 2002

First published 2002

ISBN 1-8408-5684-X TEACHING POETRY BOOK 1

The author asserts the moral right to be identified as the
author of this work.

British Library Cataloguing in Publication Data
A catalogue record for this book is available from the British
Library.

This book was designed and produced for Letts Educational
by Bender Richardson White, PO Box 266,
Uxbridge UB9 5NX.
Commissioned by Andrew Thraves
Project management by Kate Newport
Editing by Jennifer Smart
Cover design by Mike Pilley
Book design by Ben White
Illustrations by Pamela Hewetson, Robin Lawrie,
Peter Lubach, Jo Moore, Karen Perrins, Charlotte Stowell.
Production by Kerry Smith
Printed and bound in the UK by Ashford Colour Press

ACKNOWLEDGEMENTS

The publishers gratefully acknowledge the following for permission
to reproduce copyright material. Every effort has been made to
trace copyright holders, but in some cases it has proved impossi-
ble. The publishers would be happy to hear from any copyright
holder that has not been acknowledged.

Extract from 'The Bug Chant' by Tony Mitton. First printed in
Minibeasts poems chosen by Brian Moses, and published by
Macmillan in 1999. Copyright © Tony Mitton. Reprinted with the
kind permission of the author.

'Cats' by Eleanor Farjeon, from Blackbird Has Spoken published by
Macmillan. Reprinted by permission of David Higham Associates
Limited.

'Tree' by Jenny Bolt, from Green Umbrella published by A & C
Black. Reprinted by permission of the publishers.

'I Don't Like Custard' by Michael Rosen, from Early Years Poems and
Rhymes compiled by Jill Bennett, and published by Scholastic
Limited. © Michael Rosen. Reprinted by permission of Scholastic
Limited.

'Helping' by Lucy Coats, from First Rhymes by Lucy Coats, first pub-
lished in the UK by Orchard Books in 1994, a division of The Watts
Publishing Group Limited, 96 Leonard Street, London EC2A 4XD.
Reprinted by permission of the publishers.

'Sing a Song of People' by Lois Lenski, reprinted by permission of
Steven Covey, c/o Moses & Singer LLP, New York.

'Mud' by Ann Bonner, from Twinkle, Twinkle Chocolate Bar edited
by John Foster, published by OUP in 1991. © Ann Bonner.
Reprinted with the kind permission of the author.

'Ogre' by Jean Kenward, from Early Years Poems and Rhymes compiled by Jill Bennett, and published by Scholastic Limited. © Jean
Kenward. Reprinted with the kind permission of the author.

'Meddling Muddle' by Wendy Larmont, from A Blue Poetry
Paintbox. © Wendy Larmont. Reprinted with the kind permission of
the author.

Contents

The Wind

Before you begin

Can you see the wind?
Can you hear the wind? What noise does the wind make?
What sort of things does the wind do when it blows?

The Wind

The wind blows the clouds.

The wind blows the tree.

The wind blows the kite.

The wind blows the sea.

The wind blows the washing.

The wind blows me!

Reading

1. Name something the wind blows beginning with:
   a) c   b) t   c) k   d) s   e) w   f) m

2. How can you tell when the wind is blowing?

3. How can the wind help us?

4. What damage can the wind do?

5. a) What do we call a gentle wind?
   b) What do we call a very strong wind?

Writing

1. Copy the rhyme. Fill in the gaps with your own words.

   The wind blows the_____.

   The wind blows the tree.

   The wind blows the_____.

   The wind blows the sea.

   The wind blows the_____.

   The wind blows me!

2. Change some words in the rhyme and make a new rhyme.
   Replace 'The wind blows' with 'The sun shines'.
   Keep everything else the same.
   Begin your rhyme like:

   The sun shines on the clouds.

   The sun shines on the tree.

3. Use copymaster 1 to make up your own poem about the wind.

I Can Tie my Shoelace

Before you begin

Can you stand on your head?
Can you ride a bike?
Can you whistle?
What interesting things can you do?

I Can Tie my Shoelace

I can tie my shoelace.

I can comb my hair.

I can wash my hands and face.

And dry myself with care.

I can brush my teeth, too,

And do up my buttons as well.

I can say, "How do you do?"

When someone rings our bell.

Reading

1. Name something in the poem that you can do.

2. Who taught the child to do all the things in the poem?

3. How old do you think the child in the poem is?

4. Which of the things do you think is the most difficult to do?

5. Find a word in the poem that rhymes with:
   a) shoelace   b) hair   c) too   d) well

Writing

1. List five interesting things that you have learned to do.

2. Copy and complete this rhyme in your own words.
   Fill in each gap with something you can do.
   Draw some pictures showing some of the things you can do.

   I can _____.

   I can _____.

   I can run along.

   I can _____.

   I can _____.

   I can sing a song.

3. Write five things you:
   a) use your hands for   b) use your feet for   c) use your mouth for.

4. Use copymaster 2 to make up your own poem about
   things you can do.

I Like to Play on my Big Bass Drum

Before you begin

Do you like music?
What musical instruments do you like to play?
What sounds do different instruments make?

I Like to Play on my Big Bass Drum

I like to play my big bass drum,
And this is the music to it –
Boom, boom, boom
goes my big bass drum,
And that's the way I do it.

I like to play my tambourine,
And this is the music to it –
Rattle, rattle, rattle
goes my tambourine,
And that's the way I do it.

I like to play on my guitar,
And this is the music to it –
Twang, twang, twang
goes my guitar,
And that's the way I do it.

Reading

1. a) What is the first instrument that is mentioned?
   b) What noise does it make?

2. a) What is the second instrument that is mentioned?
   b) What noise does it make?

3. a) What is the third instrument that is mentioned?
   b) What noise does it make?

4. What is your favourite musical instrument? Why?

Writing

1. Write the names of three other musical instruments and the noises they make. Do it like this:

   A piano goes plink, plink, plink.

2. Write some more verses for the rhyme about other musical instruments. Do it like this:

   I like to play my long, thin flute,
   And this is the music to it –
   Toot, toot, toot
   goes my long, thin flute,
   And that's the way I do it.

3. Copy this rhyme. Finish it in your own words.

   Ding dong! Ding dong!   *Sing song! Sing song!*

   All the bells are ringing.   *All the birds are singing.*

   Ding dong! Ding dong!   _____

   Ringing all the day.   _____

4. Use copymaster 3 to make up a poem about noises wild animals make.

Ten Little Monkeys

Before you begin

The rhyme below is called a counting rhyme.
Do you know any other counting rhymes?

Ten Little Monkeys

One little monkey swings in a tree.

Two little monkeys drinking tea.

Three little monkeys play on a swing.

Four little monkeys dance and sing.

Five little monkeys jump on cars.

Six little monkeys look at the stars.

Seven little monkeys chase some cats.

Eight little monkeys wear funny hats.

Nine little monkeys nodding their heads.

Ten little monkeys asleep in their beds.

Reading

1. What did:
   a) two monkeys do?   b) five monkeys do?   c) eight monkeys do?

2. How many monkeys:
   a) played on a swing?   b) looked at the stars?   c) nodded their heads?

3. Which word in the poem rhymes with:
   a) tree   b) swing   c) cars   d) cats   e) heads?

4. Why do you think this is called a counting rhyme?

Writing

1. Rewrite the rhyme, but change the word 'monkey' to another animal.

2. Copy and complete this number rhyme in your own words.

   Number one, _____ out your tongue.
   Number _____, take off your shoe.
   Number three, bend your _____.
   Number four, _____ the door.
   Number _____, learn to jive.
   Number six, pick up _____.
   Number _____, point to heaven.
   Number eight, shut the _____.
   Number nine, hang the washing on the _____.
   Number _____, start all over again!

3. Copy and complete this counting rhyme.

   Five little mice came out to play.
   They gathered some crumbs along the way.
   Out sprang a big cat
   Sleek and black –
   Four little mice went scampering back.

   Four little mice came out to play. etc.

4. Use copymaster 4 to make up your own counting rhyme.

On Monday . . .

Before you begin

Can you name the days of the week, in order?

On Monday . . .

On Monday Jenny Jar drove her car.
Yes, Jenny Jar drove her car.

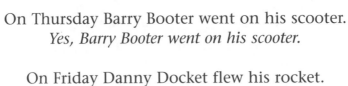

On Tuesday Simon Stoat sailed his boat.
Yes, Simon Stoat sailed his boat.

On Wednesday Debbie Drain travelled by train.
Yes, Debbie Drain travelled by train.

On Thursday Barry Booter went on his scooter.
Yes, Barry Booter went on his scooter.

On Friday Danny Docket flew his rocket.
Yes, Danny Docket flew his rocket.

On Saturday Harriet Hammel rode her camel.
Yes, Harriet Hammel rode her camel.

On Sunday they all stayed in bed, instead!
Yes, they all stayed in bed, instead!

Reading

1. What happened on:
   a) Monday?   b) Wednesday?   c) Saturday?

2. Who:
   a) rowed his boat?   b) scooted his scooter?   c) zoomed up in a rocket?

3. What was different on Sunday?

4. How many verses are there in the poem?

5. What do you notice about the second line of each verse?

Writing

1. Write how you think each of these people travelled:
   a) David Dike   b) Roberta Roach   c) Terry Tan
   d) Lucy Lip   e) Gary Gorse   f) Betty Berry
   Do it like this:

   David Dike rode a bike.

2. Write your own poem about the people above.
   Do it like the poem opposite.
   Begin like this:

   On Monday David Dike rode his bike.
   Yes, David Dike rode his bike.

3. Make up a poem about the worst week you have ever had!
   It does not have to be true! Set it out like this:

   On Monday I crashed my bike.
   Yes, I crashed my bike.

   On Tuesday I was chased by a wild lion.
   Yes, I was chased by a wild lion.

4. Use copymaster 5 to help you write about 'A Day in My Life'.

Simon Says

Before you begin

What games do you like playing at parties?
Have you ever played 'Simon Says'?

Simon Says

Simon says, "Point to your nose."

Simon says, "Touch your toes."

Simon says, "Wave your hand."

Simon says, "Dance to the band."

Simon says, "Count one, two, three."

Simon says, "Buzz like a bee."

Simon says, "It's time to hop."

We all say, "It's time to stop!"

Reading

1. What does Simon say:
   a) first?   b) second?   c) third?   d) fourth?

2. How many does Simon say to count to?

3. What does Simon say to buzz like?

4. What does Simon say it is time to do?

5. Why do you think everyone says that it is time to stop?

6. Write the word that rhymes with:
   a) nose   b) hand   c) three   d) hop

Writing

1. Copy and complete this rhyme in your own words.

   Simon says, "Catch the ball."
   Simon says, "Jump over the _____."
   Simon says, "Brush your hair."
   Simon says, "Sit on a _____."
   Simon says, "Nod your head."
   Simon says, "It's time for _____."

2. Copy and complete this rhyme in your own words. Do the actions, too!

   I can walk on tip-toe, as quiet as a mouse.
   I can stamp up the stairs in my _____.
   I can hop along like a kangaroo.
   I can go slowly like an elephant in a _____.
   I can jump so high just like a flea.
   I can splash my feet in the _____.

3. Use copymaster 6 to help you make up an animal action rhyme.

Mangoes

Before you begin

What is your favourite fruit?
What sort of fruit grows on trees?
The rhyme below is about fruit which grows on trees in the Caribbean.
Have you ever tasted any of the fruits mentioned?

Mangoes

Mangoes ripe an' juicy,
Hangin' from de tree,
Mangoes ripe an' juicy,
Go pick one for me.

Pawpaws ripe an' juicy,
Hangin' from de tree,
Papaws ripe an' juicy,
Go pick one for me.

Guavas ripe an' juicy,
Hangin' from de tree,
Guavas ripe an' juicy,
Go pick one for me.

Star-fruit ripe an' juicy,
Hangin' from de tree,
Star-fruit ripe an' juicy,
Go pick one for me.

Reading

1. Which fruit begins with:
   a) g?   b) m?   c) p?   d) s?

2. Which fruit is mentioned in the:
   a) first verse?   b) second verse?   c) third verse?   d) last verse?

3. Do the fruits in the rhyme grow in the ground or on a tree?

4. Copy and complete this sentence.
   All the fruits are ripe and _____.

5. Where do all the fruits come from?

6. a) How many verses are there in the rhyme?
   b) How many lines are there in each verse?

Writing

1. Write the names of four other fruits that grow on a tree.

2. Now make up some more verses of your own for the rhyme.
   Use the names of the fruit you thought of in your verses.

3. Copy this counting rhyme from the Caribbean.
   Write some more verses for it.

> *Five biscuits in a pack.*
> *If you want one turn your back.*
> *Back to back, sago pap,*
> *Five biscuits in a pack.*
>
> *Four biscuits in a pack etc...*

4. Use copymaster 7 to help you write a rhyme about going to market.

Here is the Ostrich

Before you begin

Have you ever seen an ostrich? What does it look like?
Have you ever seen a hedgehog? What does it look like?

Here is the Ostrich

Here is the ostrich, straight and tall.

It nods its head above us all.

Here is a long snake on the ground.

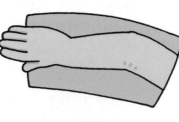

It slithers along with a hissing sound.

Here is a bird that flies so high.

It flaps its wings up in the sky.

Here is a hedgehog. It's prickly and small.

It rolls itself into a ball.

Here is a spider. It's crawls on your bed.

It crawls up the wall and back to its web.

Here are the children fast asleep.

And here is a night owl having a peep.

18

Reading

1. Which word rhymes with:
   a) tall?   b) ground?   c) high?   d) asleep?

2. Which animal:
   a) nods its head?   b) makes a hissing sound?   c) flaps its wings?
   d) rolls itself into a ball?   e) crawls back to its web?

3. Are the children awake or asleep?

4. What sort of bird has a peep at the children?

Writing

1. Use the words in the box to help you make up a rhyme.

   | creep   peep   sweep   sleep |

   With my broom I sweep, sweep, sweep.

   On my toes I _____, _____, _____.

   With my eyes I _____, _____, _____.

   In my bed I _____, _____, _____.

2. Copy and complete this rhyme. Make up some actions to go with it.

   Little Robin Redbreast sat upon a rail,

   Niddle noddle went his head and wag wag went his tail.

   _____ _____ went his head and _____ _____ went his tail,

   As Little _____ _____ sat upon a _____.

3. Use copymaster 8 to make a rhyme about cooking.

In the Fields

Before you begin

How many different farm animals can you name?
What noise does each animal make?

In the Fields

One day I saw a big brown cow
Raise her head and chew,
I said, "Good morning, Mrs Cow,"
But all she said was, "Moo!"

One day I saw a woolly lamb,
I followed it quite far,
I said, "Good morning, little lamb,"
But all it said was, "Baa!"

One day I saw a big brown horse
Munching a bag of hay,
I said, "Good morning, Mr Horse,"
But all it said was, "Neigh!"

Reading

1. Which animal was seen:
   a) first?   b) second?   c) third?

2. a) What sort of cow was it?   b) What noise did it make?

3. a) What sort of lamb was it?   b) What noise did it make?

4. a) What sort of horse was it?   b) What noise did it make?

5. a) How many verses are there?
   b) How many lines are there in each verse?

Writing

1. What noises do the following animals make?
   a) duck   b) hen   c) donkey   d) dog   e) mouse   f) cat

2. Copy and complete two more verses for the rhyme.

   One day I saw a little white duck,

   Walking along the track.

   I said, "Good morning, little duck,"

   But all it said was, "_____!"

   One day I saw a fat brown hen,

   What a stroke of luck!

   I said, "_____,"

   But all it said was, "_____!"

3. Choose another animal and make up another verse of your own.

4. Use copymaster 9 to write a rhyme about farm animals.

The Bug Chant

Before you begin

Try saying this tongue-twister as quickly as you can a few times,
before you read the 'Bug Chant':

I'm as snug as a bug in a rug.
Can you hug a slug in a mug?

The Bug Chant

Red bugs, bed bugs,
find them on your head bugs.

Green bugs, mean bugs,
lanky, long and lean bugs.

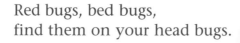

Pink bugs, sink bugs,
swimming in your drink bugs.

Yellow bugs, mellow bugs,
lazy little fellow bugs.

White bugs, night bugs,
buzzing round the light bugs.

Black bugs, slack bugs,
climbing up your back bugs.

Blue bugs, goo bugs,
find them in your shoe bugs.

Extract from poem by Tony Mitton

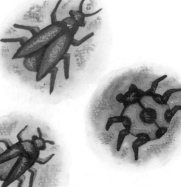

Reading

1. a) What is the title of the rhyme?   b) Who wrote it?

2. Find a word that rhymes with:
   a) red   b) green   c) pink   d) yellow
   e) white f) black   g) blue

3. Copy down your favourite verse.

4. Say something you liked about the rhyme.

Writing

1. Here are some other verses from the rhyme. Copy them and fill in what you think the missing words might be.

   Thin bugs, _____ bugs,
   hiding in your hat bugs.

   Big bugs, small bugs,
   crawling on your _____ bugs.

   Smooth bugs, hairy bugs,
   flying like a _____ bugs.

2. Copy and finish this well-known chanting rhyme.

   One, two, three, four, five,

   Once I caught a _____ alive.

   Six, seven, _____, _____, _____,

   Then I let it _____.

   Why did you let it go?

   Because _____.

   Which finger did it _____?

   This _____ _____ on the right.

3. Use copymaster 10 to help you make up your own skipping rhyme.

If I Were . . .

If you could be any animal what would you be?
What sort of things would you do?

If I Were

If I were a bird, high in the sky,
I would flap my wings and fly, fly, fly.

If I were a dog going for a run,
I would wag my tail and have some fun.

If I were a mouse in a hole in the ground,
I would come right out and scamper around.

If I were a frog, all on my own,
I would hop along from stone to stone.

Reading

1. Which animal is in the:
   a) first verse?   b) second verse?   c) third verse?   d) fourth verse?

2. What would you do if you were:
   a) a bird?   b) a dog?   c) a mouse?   d) a frog?

3. Write a word that rhymes with:
   a) sky   b) run   c) ground   d) own

4. a) How many verses are there?
   b) How many lines are there in each verse?

Writing

1. Copy and complete some more verses in your own words.

   If I were a horse I would gallop down the lane,

   I would turn around and do it _____.

   If I were a lion I would hide behind a rock,

   I would _____ out loud and give you a shock.

   If I were a brown bear I would climb a tree,

   I would find some honey and eat it for my _____.

2. Think of some other animals you would like to be.
   Make up some more verses of your own.

3. Use copymaster 11 to write a rhyme about people you would like to be.

Pitter Patter

Do you like rain? What is good about it? What is bad about it?
What noise do raindrops make when they fall?
Do you like storms? What happens in a storm?

Rain on the House Top

Rain on the house top,
Rain on the tree,
Rain on the green grass -
But don't rain on me!

Pitter Patter

Pitter patter, pitter patter,
Pitter patter goes the rain.
Pitter patter, pitter patter,
On my window pane.

The Storm

Listen to the rain.
See the lightning flash.
Next comes the thunder.
Can you hear the crash?

Reading

1. What noise does the rain make on the window pane?

2. What are the first two poems about?

3. What is the third poem about?

4. What does lightning do?

5. What does thunder do?

6. Which poem do you like best? Say why.

Writing

1. Write down as many 'noise' words about the rain as possible.
   Do it like this: plip, plop, splish, splash

2. Now write down some 'noise' words about storms.

3. Copy these two poems about storms. Think of a good word to finish
   each one.

   Plip, plop, splash.   *Zigzag, flash,*
   Plip, plop, splash.   *Zigzag, flash.*
   Plip, plop, splash,   *See the lightning zig zag.*
   Biff, bang, _____.   *Hear the thunder _____.*

4. Copy this poem and complete it in your own words.
   Try and write another verse for it.

   Rain on the hillside,
   Rain on the sea.
   Rain on the forest
   But don't rain on _____.

   Rain on the spider.
   Rain on the bee.
   Rain on the _____.
   _____.

5. Use copymaster 12 to help you write your own poem about rain.

Cats

Before you begin

Do you have a cat? What is it like? Where does it sleep?
What sort of things do cats like to do?
How do cats move?
What noises do they make?

Cats

Cats sleep
Anywhere,
Any table,
Any chair,
Top of piano,
Window-ledge,
In the middle,
On the edge,
Open drawer,
Empty shoe,
Anybody's
Lap will do,
Fitted in a
Cardboard box,
In the cupboard
With your frocks –
Anywhere!
They don't care!
Cats sleep
Anywhere.

Eleanor Farjeon

28

Reading

1. a) What is the poem called?   b) Who wrote it?

2. What is the poem all about?

3. Is it a long thin poem, or a short fat poem?

4. Write a word that rhymes with:
   a) anywhere   b) ledge   c) shoe   d) box

5. Did you like the poem? Give a reason for your answer.

Writing

1. Write some words that describe a cat's:
   a) fur   b) claws   c) tail   d) whiskers   e) teeth   f) eyes

2. Copy and complete these sentences about a cat in your own words.
   Make up some more sentences of your own.
   A cat's fur is soft and smooth.
   A cat's claws are sharp and scratchy.
   A cat's tail is _____.

3. Copy this poem about a cat and complete it in your own words.

   Pretty little tabby cat
   Sitting there upon the mat.
   Pretty little tabby cat
   Show me how you arch your back.

   Pretty little tabby cat
   Coming in through the door.
   Pretty little tabby cat
   Show me how you lick your _____.

   _____
   With fur as soft as silk.
   _____
   _____ you drink your milk.

4. Use copymaster 13 to help you make up your own poem about cats.

Jelly on the Plate

Before you begin

Say this tongue-twister as fast as you can, before you read the poem below.
Jolly jelly, juicy jelly, wibble wobble woo,
Jelly jolly, jelly juicy, how do you do!

Jelly on the Plate

Jelly on the plate,
Jelly on the plate,
Wibble, wobble,
Wibble, wobble,
Jelly on the plate.

Sausages in the pan,
Sausages in the pan,
Sizzle, sizzle,
Sizzle, sizzle,
Sausages in the pan.

Biscuits in the jar,
Biscuits in the jar,
Munch, munch,
Munch, munch,
Biscuits in the jar.

Apples in the bowl,
Apples in the bowl,
Crunch, crunch,
Crunch, crunch,
Apples in the bowl.

Reading

1. Where:
    a) is the jelly?   b) are the sausages?
    c) are the biscuits?   d) are the apples?

2. What goes: a) wibble wobble?   b) sizzle, sizzle?

3. What do you: a) munch?   b) crunch?

4. Which of the things in the poem would you like to eat best? Say why.

Writing

1. What noise do you make when:
    a) you drink milk?   b) you eat an ice cream?   c) you eat crisps?

2. What noise do eggs make when they are frying?

3. Copy these verses and use the words you thought of to complete them.

    Milk in a glass,   *Ice cream in a cone,*
    Milk in a glass,   *Ice cream in a cone,*

    _____   _____

    _____   _____
    Milk in a glass.   *Ice cream in a cone.*

    Crisps in a packet,   *Eggs in a pan,*
    Crisps in a packet,   *Eggs' in a pan,*

    _____   _____

    _____   _____
    Crisps in a packet.   *Eggs in a pan.*

4. Write another food poem.
    Fill each gap with food beginning with the same letter as the person's
    name.

    John likes juice and _____ and jam.
    Harriet likes _____ and _____ and ham.
    Polly likes _____ and _____ and peas.
    Charlie likes _____ and _____ and cheese.

5. Use copymaster 14 to help you write a poem called 'The Dragon's Dinner'

Trees

Before you begin

How many different sorts of tree can you name?
How do trees help us?
What animals and insects live in trees?

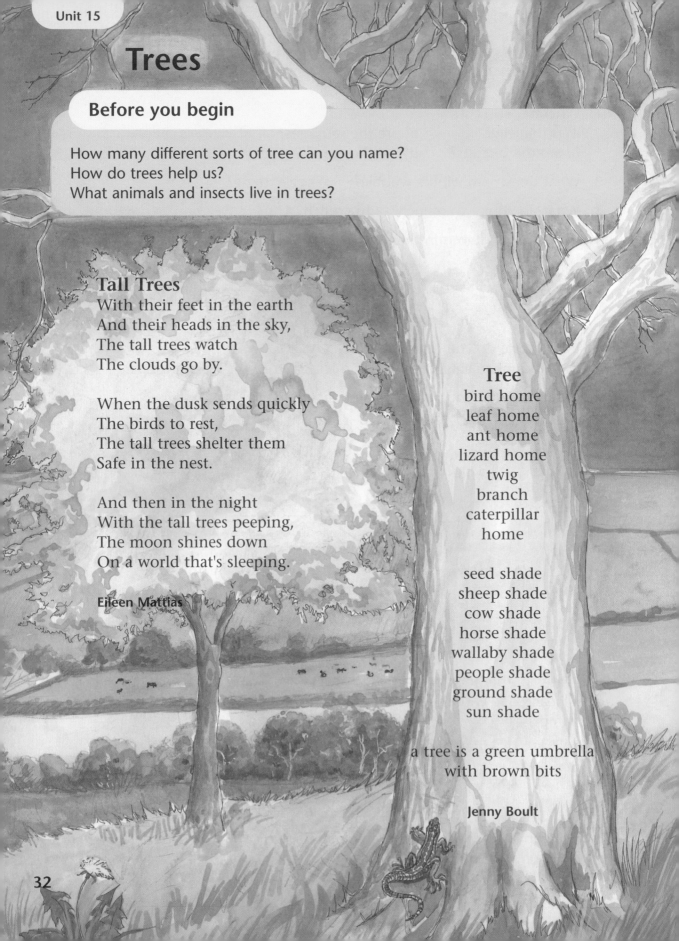

Tall Trees
With their feet in the earth
And their heads in the sky,
The tall trees watch
The clouds go by.

When the dusk sends quickly
The birds to rest,
The tall trees shelter them
Safe in the nest.

And then in the night
With the tall trees peeping,
The moon shines down
On a world that's sleeping.

Eileen Mattias

Tree
bird home
leaf home
ant home
lizard home
twig
branch
caterpillar
home

seed shade
sheep shade
cow shade
horse shade
wallaby shade
people shade
ground shade
sun shade

a tree is a green umbrella
with brown bits

Jenny Boult

32

Reading

1. What are both poems about?

2. What do you think are: a) the feet of a tree? b) the head of a tree?

3. Name some things that live in trees.

4. Name some things that a tree gives shade to.

5. How is a tree like a green umbrella?

6. Which poem did you like the best? Say why.

Writing

1. Think of the name of each part of the tree. Write and say what you think each thing is like. Do it like this:

   The trunk of the tree is its body.

   The bark of the tree is like a coat.

2. Copy this rhyme and think of a word to go in the gap.

   Sammy Lee climbed a tree.

   He fell off and scraped his _____.

3. Copy this rhyme about a tree and choose a word to go in each gap.

   When I sat in the shade of a tree,

   I looked up to see what I could _____.

   I saw a _____ and a yellow bumble _____

   And a sleepy owl looking down at _____.

4. Use copymaster 15 to help you write a poem called 'Our Tree Home.'

Mary Lost her Coat

Before you begin

Have you ever lost anything important?
What sort of things is it easy to lose?
How do you feel when you lose things?
What do you do?

Mary Lost her Coat

Mary lost her coat,
Mary lost her hat,
Mary lost her wellingtons –
Now what do you think of that?

Mary lost her dog,
Mary lost her cat,
Mary lost her guinea pig –
Now what do you think of that?

Mary lost her ball,
Mary lost her bat,
Mary lost her brand new kite –
Now what do you think of that?

Mary lost her mug,
Mary lost her mat,
Mary lost her knife and fork –
Now what do you think of that?

Reading

1. Who kept losing things in the poem?

2. What sort of girl do you think Mary was?

3. Name the things she lost in the first verse.

4. Name the things she lost in the third verse.

5. Write down all the words in the poem that rhyme with 'that'.

6. a) How many verses are there in the poem?
   b) Write something you notice that is the same in each verse.

Writing

1. Rewrite the first verse of the poem. Replace the word 'lost' in it with the word 'found'.

2. Copy and complete this poem in your own words.

   Paul lost his coat
   Paul lost his shoe.
   Paul lost his _____ and tie. –
   Now what do you think he'll do?

   Paul _____ his brush.
   Paul lost his glue.
   Paul lost his _____ and pen
   Now what _____?

   Paul lost his red crayon.
   Paul lost his blue.
   Paul lost his_____.–
   _____

   _____ old bike.
   Paul lost his bike that was new.
   _____
   _____

3. Copy the verse below. It has a similar pattern.
   Follow its pattern and make up another verse of your own.

   > *Mr Smith lost his glasses.*
   > *Mr Smith lost his van.*
   > *Mr Smith lost his book and bag. –*
   > *What a silly man!*

4. Use copymaster 16 to help you write a poem called 'A Hat for a Cat'.

Questions

Before you begin

What sort of things would you like to know more about?

Questions

How far are the stars?
How deep is the sea?
Who lives on the moon?
What's inside of me?

Why is grass green?
How does the sun shine?
What makes it thunder?
Why must I share what's mine?

Why do ants work so hard?
Why don't jellyfish have feet?
When did the world first begin?
How does my heart know when to beat?

Why do snails live in shells?
Why does a fire glow?
So many, many questions.
So much for me to know!

Reading

1. Why do we ask questions?

2. How many questions are there in the first verse?

3. Give an answer to the fourth question in verse 1.

4. Do you think most of the questions in the poem are easy or hard?

5. Which question do you think is the hardest?

6. Which word in the poem rhymes with:
   a) sea?   b) shine?   c) feet?   d) glow?

Writing

1. Write down four difficult questions you would like to ask. Make a class poem of difficult questions.

2. Copy and complete this well-known nursery rhyme which contains questions.

   Pussy cat, pussy cat, where have you been?

   _____

   Pussy cat, pussy cat, what did you there?

   _____

3. The answers to the questions below rhyme – but they are nonsense! Copy the questions again and write some nonsense answers of your own. Make them rhyme.

What's your name?	*Just The Same.*
Where are you from?	*Ping Pong.*
What's your address?	*Watercress.*
What's your number?	*Cucumber.*
Where do you shop?	*Bottle of pop.*
What do you eat?	*My bed sheet.*
What do you drink?	*Nod and wink.*
Who is your friend?	*Round the bend.*
What time do you go to bed?	*Bang my head.*

4. Use copymaster 17 to help you write 'An Alphabet of Animal Questions'

Noise

Noise

Ben is blowing a trumpet;
Amy is banging a drum;
Mary is shouting at Emma;
Dan has bashed his thumb.
Sarah is singing a pop song;
Tommy is whistling a tune.
There so much noise around me –
I do hope it gets quiet soon!

Reading

1. Who is:
   a) blowing a trumpet?   b) banging a drum?   c) shouting?
   d) singing?   e) whistling?

2. What has Dan done?

3. Which word rhymes with:
   a) drum?   b) tune?

4. Does the person who wrote the poem like noise? How can you tell?

Writing

1. Write down what noises these things make. The first is done for you.
   a) steam *hiss*   b) scissors   c) a clock   d) a church bell
   e) horse's hooves   f) coins in a purse   g) the brakes of a car
   h) old hinges on a door   i) sausages frying in a pan
   j) Christmas crackers

2. Make a poem of LOUD noises. It does not have to rhyme. Do it like this:

   > *Doors SLAM.*
   > *Motorbikes ROAR.*

3. Now make up a poem of QUIET noises. Do it like this:

   > *Cats purr.*
   > *Water drips.*

4. Copy the first verse of this poem about town noises.
   Follow the same pattern and write some more verses about:
   a) the buses in the garage   b) the boats in the harbour
   c) the planes at the airport.

   > *Come down to the station early in the morning,*
   > *See all the railway trains standing in a row.*
   > *See all the drivers starting up their engines.*
   > *Clicketty-clack and off they go!*

5. Use copymaster 18 to help you write a poem called 'Car Noises'.

I Don't Like Custard

Before you begin

What is your favourite food?
Is there any food you really hate?

I Don't Like Custard

I don't like custard
I don't like custard

Sometimes it's lumpy
sometimes it's thick
I don't care what it's like
It always makes me sick

I don't like custard
I don't like custard

Don't want it on my pie
don't want it on my cake
don't want it on my pudding
don't want it on my plate

I don't like custard
I don't like custard

It dribbles on the table
It dribbles on the floor
It sticks on your fingers
Then it sticks to the door

I don't like custard
I don't like custard

I can't eat it slowly
I can't eat it quick
Any way I eat it
It always makes me sick

I don't like custard
I don't like custard

Michael Rosen

Reading

1. a) What is the poem called?
   b) Who wrote it?

2. The poet says that:
   a) custard is lumpy and _____.
   b) custard dribbles on the table and _____.
   c) custard makes him _____.

3. How many times does the poet say that he does not like custard?

4. Did you like the poem? Say why (or why not).

Writing

1. Match up the beginning and ending of each rhyming sentence. Write them in your excercise book.

   I don't like custard ------------   or sitting still.
   I don't like going to bed   or going too high.
   I don't like the smell of paint   or boss me about.
   I don't like people who lie   or standing on my head.
   I don't like people who shout   or eating mustard.
   I don't like being ill   or when I faint.

2. Copy and complete this poem.
   Each line must end with something to eat or drink, and must rhyme.

   I don't like mice but I do like rice.
   I don't like poodles but I do like _____.
   I don't like silk but I do like _____.
   I don't like parrots but I do like _____.
   I don't like to scream but I do like _____.
   I don't like pips but I do like _____.
   I don't like stew but I do like YOU!

3. Use copymaster 19 to write a poem called 'Who Likes…?'

Helping

Before you begin

What sort of things can you do to help at home?

Helping

Powder, bubbles, splish splash sploshing,
Helping Mum to do the washing.
Wind must blow and sun must shine,
Hang the washing on the line.
Spray the dirt off, scrub the muck,
Helping Daddy clean his truck.
Peel the carrots, chop, chop, crunch,
Helping Mum to make the lunch.
Drying up goes clink, clank, clink,
Helping Daddy at the sink.
Dig my fork in, pull up weeds,
Helping Mum to sow her seeds.
Cheese and eggs and krispiepops,
Helping Daddy at the shops.
Tea and toast and milk and bread,
In the bath and off to bed.
Rain, or cloud or frosty weather,
We all like to help together.

Lucy Coats

Reading

1. List some of the things the child did to help Mum.

2. List some of the things the child did to help Daddy.

3. Write a word that rhymes with:
   a) sploshing   b) shine   c) muck   d) crunch   e) clink
   f) weeds   g) shops   h) bread   i) weather

4. Say something you liked about the poem.

5. List some jobs you can do to help at school.

Writing

1. Write what job you think each person does to help.
   Their jobs rhyme with their names. The first one is done for you.

   a) Mrs Proctor is a doctor.   b) Mrs Meacher is my _____.
   c) Mr Corry drives a _____.   d) Miss Beaner is a _____.
   e) Mr Most delivers the _____.   f) Mrs Heath looks after my _____.
   g) Miss Mop serves in a _____.   h) Mr Dubbish collects our _____.

2. Copy this poem about cleaning up. Write each line where it should go.

> I must wash the dishes and pick up Ted.
> I must check how nice my house looks!
> I must sweep up the rubbish and tip it in.
> I must straighten the cushions where I last sat.

I must get a brush. I must get a bin.

_____

I must mop the floor. I must make my bed.

_____

I must clean the bath. I must hoover the mat.

_____

I must do the washing. I must tidy my books.

_____

3. Use copymaster 20 to help you write a poem about helping.

The Holiday Train

Before you begin

Have you ever been on a train? What was it like?

The Holiday Train

Here is the train!
Here is the train!
Let us get in!
Let us get in!

Where shall we sit?
Where shall we sit?
When will it go?
When will it go?

What does it say?
What does it say?
"Let us get on!"
"Let us get on!"

Look at the trees!
Look at the trees!
See all the cows!
See all the cows!

Isn't it fun?
Isn't it fun?
Going along!
Going along!

Hurrying on!
Hurrying on!
Nearly there!
Nearly there!

Look at the sea!
Look at the sea!
See all the ships!
See all the ships!

Here we are!
Here we are!
Out we get!
Out we get!

Irene Thompson

Reading

1. Where are the children going on a train?

2. What things did they see out of the window?

3. Why do you think the poem is called 'The Holiday Train'?

4. a) How many verses are there?
   b) How many lines are there in each verse?
   c) Why do you think each line is repeated?

5. Say something you liked about the poem.

Writing

1. What do you think the children will do when they get off the train at the seaside? Continue the poem. Make up some verses of your own.
   Do it like this:

   > *Sun's very hot!*
   > *Sun's very hot!*
   > *Onto the sand!*
   > *Onto the sand!*

2. Imagine going for a ride on different things. Copy and complete the first verse of this poem. Make up two more verses of your own.

   > *Aeroplanes, aeroplanes all in a row;*
   > *Aeroplanes, aeroplanes ready to _____.*
   > *Hear all the engines beginning to roar,*
   > *Get on quick and shut the _____.*
   > *Flying, flying up into the sky.*
   > *Faster and faster, ever so _____.*
   >
   > *Coaches, coaches, all in a row ...*
   >
   > *Boats, boats, all in a row ...*

3. Use copymaster 21 to help you write a poem called 'Row, Row, Row your Boat'.

Sing a Song of People

Before you begin

What sort of things do you see in a busy town centre?
What do you hear? What do you smell?

Sing a Song of People

Sing a song of people
Walking fast or slow;
People in the city
Up and down they go.

People on the sidewalk,
People on the bus;
People passing, passing,
In back and front of us.
People on the subway
Underneath the ground;
People riding taxis
Round and round and round.

People with their hats on,
Going in the doors;
People with umbrellas
When it rains and pours.
People in tall buildings
And in stores below;
Riding elevators
Up and down they go.

People walking singly,
People in a crowd;
People saying nothing,
People talking loud.
People laughing, smiling,
Grumpy people, too;
People who just hurry
And never look at you!

Sing a song of people
Who like to come and go;
Sing of city people
You see but never know!

Lois Lenski

Reading

1. What is the poem all about?

2. Write three things some of the people in the poem are doing.

3. Is the poem about a quiet town or a busy city?

4. How can you tell the city is in another country?

5. a) What is a subway?   b) What are elevators?

6. Write a word that rhymes with:
   a) slow   b) ground   c) doors   d) crowd

Writing

1. Write a list of five things in town you would: a) see b) hear c) smell

2. Copy the first verse of the poem.
   Use it to help you complete the other verses.

   This is the way the bus drivers drive – stop, start, go, stop, start, go.
   This is the way the bus drivers drive – stop, start, go, all day long.

   This is the way the people shop – hurry, look, spend, hurry, look, spend …

   This is the way the cars all go …

   This is the way the lifts all go …

3. Copy and complete this poem in your own words.

   Tall buildings in town, lifts going up and _____.
   Doors swinging round about, people walking in and _____.
   Buses stopping at the stops, people popping into _____.
   Lots of traffic, lots of noise, lots of girls and lots of _____.
   Offices, factories, a library, too, different animals in the _____.
   Letter boxes, street lights – too much to see, too many _____!

4. Use copymaster 22 to help you write a poem called 'Eeny Meeny'.

Mud

Before you begin

What makes it muddy?
Do you like playing in mud?

Mud

Take a bucket of soil.
Some water from a can.
Mix them well
in an old saucepan.
Add a few leaves.
Some flower petals too.
And soon you'll have
A Mudpie stew.

Take slugs and snails,
a scattering of sand.
Rub them round
with your muddy hand.
Leave in the sun
a while to bake.
And soon you'll have
A Mudpie cake.

Ann Bonner

Reading

1. What is the title of the poem called?

2. Who wrote the poem?

3. Write a word that rhymes with:
   a) can   b) too   c) sand   d) bake

4. List some of the things used to make a Mudpie stew and Mudpie cake.

5. How does the sun help?

6. Did you like the poem? Say why.

Writing

1. Copy and complete this poem.

   See the ducks waddling down the lane.
   Waddle, waddle, quack! Waddle, waddle, quack!
   Waddling through the mud and _____.
   Waddle, waddle, quack! _____!
   They're going to the _____ and back again.
   Waddle, _____! _____!

2. Copy and complete this poem about a crocodile in your own words.

   If you should meet a crocodile,
   In a muddy puddle,
   Don't stop to say hello
   Or ask him for a cuddle.

   If _____,
   In a muddy bog,
   Take care _____ he's full of guile –
   _____ than a frog!

   If you should meet a crocodile,
   Don't get a stick and poke him,
   Ignore his lovely welcoming smile.
   And be careful not to _____ him.

   If _____,
   Who seems to be getting _____,
   Don't stop to _____ for a little while
   Or _____ for his dinner!

3. Use copymaster 23 to help you write a poem called 'Hubble Bubble Muddy Puddle'.

Ogre

Ogre

I like cabbage
I like plums
I like everything
that comes.

I like minnows
I like whales,
I like a tool bag
full of nails.

I like snow
and I like ice –
I could eat
a mountain twice.

I like rubbish,
boxes, bins,
empty bottles,
knitting pins.

I like gravel,
I like stones,
I like heaps of
elephants' bones.

I can eat
as much as ten –
half the world,
and half again.

If all the seas
were in one cup,
I could swallow –
and drink them up!

Jean Kenward

Reading

1. a) What is the poem called?   b) Think of another title of your own.

2. Who wrote the poem?

3. What is the poem all about?

4. a) How many verses are there?
    b) How many lines are there in each verse?

5. Find a word that rhymes with:
    a) plums   b) whales   c) ice   d) bins   e) stones   f) ten   g) cup

6. Did you like the poem? Say why.

Writing

1. Write down as many words as you can to describe how a giant:
    a) looks   b) walks   c) talks   d) eats

2. Complete this poem about what a giant eats. Each line must rhyme.

> A giant eats:
> some cans and some vans,
> some stars and some _____,
> some trains and some _____,
> some fridges and some _____,
> some socks and some _____,
> some brollies and some _____,
> some pails and some _____,
> some plugs and some _____,
> some zips and some _____,
> … and then he sleeps!

3. Use copymaster 24 to help you write a poem called 'Who's That?'

Little Pony

Before you begin

Children enjoy poetry all over the world.
These two poems come from different parts of the world.
'Little Pony' comes from the Middle East.
'Pussy in de Moonlight' comes from the Caribbean.

Little Pony

I had a little pony,
He wouldn't go anywhere,
Till he heard the Muezzin
Calling us to prayer;
Then clip-clop, clip-clop,
To the Mosque we'd go,
Summer and winter,
Sunshine or snow.

Pussy in de Moonlight

Pussy in de moonlight
Pussy in de zoo
Pussy never come home
Till half past two.

Reading

1. Where does each poem come from?

2. What was the pony waiting for before he would move?

3. Where did the pony go?

4. Did the pony mind what the weather was like?

5. Was it night or day in the second poem? How can you tell?

6. What time did the cat get home?

7. Look at copymaster 25 for some more poems from around the world.

Writing

1. Copy this poem and fill in the missing words.
   When you have finished, make up another verse of your own.

   I had a little horse,
   He wouldn't move at all,
   Till he saw Humpty Dumpty
   Fall off the _____.

   I had a little donkey,
   He wouldn't move a pace,
   Till I gave him some water
   So he could wash his _____.

   I had a little camel,
   He wouldn't move a jot,
   Till I gave him some curry
   That was very _____.

   I had a little oxen,
   He wouldn't move or go,
   Till the weather turned cold
   And it began to _____.

2. Copy and finish off this poem in your own words.
   When you have finished, make up some more verses of your own.

   Pussy in de starlight
   Pussy in de tree
   Pussy never come home
   Till half past three.

   Pussy in de thunderstorm
   Pussy on de drive

   _____
   _____

   Pussy in de sunshine
   Pussy on the floor

   _____
   _____

   Pussy in de fog and gloom
   Pussy in de sticks

   _____
   _____

Betty's Butter

Before you begin

Can you guess why the verses below are called tongue-twisters?

Betty's Butter

Betty bought a bit of butter.
Betty said, "My butter's bitter.
If I put it in my batter,
It will make my batter bitter.
I'd better buy some better butter."
So she bought a bit of butter
Better than her bitter butter,
When she put it in her batter,
It made Betty's batter better.

Swan Swam

Swan swam over the sea –
Swim, swan, swim!
Swan swam back again –
Well swum, swan!

Reading

1. What did Betty buy?

2. What was wrong with Betty's butter?

3. What did Betty do to make her batter better?

4. Where did swan swim?

5. Why are these rhymes called tongue-twisters?

6. Copymaster 26 contains more tongue-twisters for you to read and enjoy.

Writing

1. Write what you think each of the children below like to do.
   Try and begin lots of words in each sentence with the same letter.
   The first one is done for you.
   a) Lily likes to lick lollies.   b) Sam   c) Ben   d) Tara   e) Polly

2. Copy these sentences. Work out the missing letter in each sentence.

   _ig _oys _uy _lue _alloons.

   _ood _irls _ather _reen _rapes.

   _an _ats _atch _olds?

   _our _at _rogs _ound _ive _lying _ish.

3. Copy this tongue-twister. Fill in the missing words.

   The hairdresser's clippers went clip, clip, clip.
   The hairdresser's snippers went snip, _____, _____.
   Clip went the clippers.
   Snip went _____.
   Clip, clip clippers,
   Snip _____.
   Click, snip, click, snip, click, snip, click!

On the Wall

Before you begin

Lots of rhymes and poems have fun with sounds.
The first rhyme uses the same letter sound several times.
The second rhyme uses words which tell us about sounds.

On the Wall

A big brown bumblebee
Sat on a wall.
It said it could hum
And that was all.

Clip, Clop

Clip, clop, clip, clop,
The horse trots down the lane.
Clip, clop, clip, clop,
The horse trots back again.

Reading

1. The first line of 'On the Wall' uses the same letter to begin three words. What letter is it?

2. Which insect is named in 'On the Wall'?

3. What did the bumblebee say it could do?

4. The second rhyme uses words which tell us about sounds. Which words are these?

5. Which animal is named in the second rhyme?

6. Where is the horse going?

Writing

1. Write ten interesting words beginning with 'b'.

2. Copy and complete these verses in your own words.

A wet wiggly worm
Sat on the wall.
It said it could _____
And that was all.

A fine fat frog
Sat on the wall.
_____
_____

A beautiful blue butterfly
Sat on the wall.
_____
_____

A single silver snake
Sat on the wall.
_____
_____

3. Copy and complete these verses for the second rhyme in your own words.

Trimp, tramp, trimp, tramp,
The elephant tramps down the track.
_____
_____

Hip, hop, hip, hop,
The frog hops down the road.
_____
_____

4. Use copymaster 27 to help you write a poem using 'sound' words.

I Had a Little Brother

Before you begin

Some poems don't make sense.
They are called nonsense poems.
They are written to make us laugh.

I Had a Little Brother

I had a little brother
No bigger than my thumb.
I put him in the coffee pot.
He rattled like a drum.

I had a little sister
No bigger than a flea.
I put her in the milk jug
Then poured her in my tea.

As I Was Going Out One Day

As I was going out one day
My head fell off and rolled away.
But when I saw that it was gone,
I picked it up and put it on.

And when I got into the street
A fellow cried, "Look at your feet!"
I looked at them and sadly said,
"I've left them both asleep in bed!"

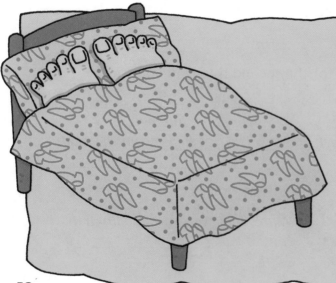

Reading

1. What are nonsense poems?

2. What happened to your little brother when you put him in a coffee pot?

3. What happened to your little sister when you put her in a milk jug?

4. What fell off when you went out one day?

5. Where did you leave your feet?

6. Which poem do you like best? Say why.

7. There are more nonsense rhymes to enjoy on copymaster 28.

Writing

1. Finish these rhyming sentences about people who can be found in your house. Make up some of your own, too. Make them as silly as you like.

> Mr Mop can skip and hop.
> Mr Tap wears a _____.
> Mr Stool is a _____.
> Mr Chair has curly _____.

2. Copy and complete these verses in your own words. Make up some of your own when you have finished them.

> I've got a dog.
> Her name is Bet.
> When it rains
> She always gets wet.

> I've got a dog.
> His name is Pete.
> My dog Pete
> Has smelly _____.

> I've got a dog.
> His name is Ben.
>
> _____
> _____

> I've got a dog.
> Her name is Nellie.
>
> _____
> _____

3. Write a nonsense rhyme of your own.
   Copy and complete the first two verses to start you off.

> Who's that under the table?
> Have a look. It's Aunty Mabel.

> Who's that wearing a woolly hat?
> Have a look. _____.

Meddling Muddle

Before you begin

Some poems tell stories. What do you think this poem is about?

Meddling Muddle

"Don't touch that Magic Spell Book!"
The wizard warned the boy.
"Just get on with the sweeping,
I'm off to see King Roy."

The wizard left the workshop.
The boy rushed up the stair.
He rummaged through the bookcase
And found the spellbook there.

He turned the pages quickly
To find the Brushing Spell.
He chanted all the verses.
He thought that all was well.

And then he started shrinking!
He got a dreadful fright.
He'd cast the spell so quickly
He hadn't said it right.

The wizard came back later.
He peered around the door.
The boy had disappeared.
A mouse was on the floor.

"You foolish little creature!
You've meddled with my book.
I'll have to turn you back again.
Now. Let me take a look."

He pulled the cloak around him
And counted up to ten.
There was a bolt of lightning!
The boy stood there again.

"Now let that be a lesson."
The wizard's voice was cold.
"NEVER play with magic,
And do as you are told!"

Wendy Larmont

Reading

1. a) What is the poem called?   b) Who wrote it?
   c) How many verses does it have?
   d) How many lines are there in each verse?

2. Whom did the wizard go to see?

3. What did the wizard tell the boy not to do?

4. What happened to the boy when the spell went wrong?

5. How did the wizard feel when he returned?

6. What lesson can we all learn from the story poem?

Writing

1. Here is a fairy story poem. The first verse is correct but the other
   verses are in the wrong order. Copy the poem and put the
   verses in the correct order.

   Verse 1   *There was a princess long ago, long ago, long ago,*
                  There was a princess long ago, long ago.

   Verse _   *A great big forest grew around, etc.*

   Verse _   *And she lived in a big high tower, etc.*

   Verse _   *One day a fairy waved her wand, etc.*

   Verse _   *They got married straight away, etc.*

   Verse _   *He took his sword and cut it down, etc.*

   Verse _   *A brave young prince came riding by, etc.*

   Verse _   *The princess slept for a hundred years, etc.*

   Verse _   *He took her hand to wake her up, etc.*

2. Use copymaster 29 to help you write a story poem called 'Old Noah's Ark'.

What Are You?

Before you begin

Some rhymes and poems try to catch you out, or make you think.
Do you know any riddles?

What Are You?

I am a gold lock;　　I am a silver lock;
I am a gold key.　　I am a silver key

I am a brass lock.　　I am a lead lock;
I am a brass lock;　　I am a lead key.

I am a monk lock:
I am a …………..!

Riddle

What kind of ants have trunks?

Reading

1. What is the answer to 'What are you?'.

2. Why do you think this is called a 'catch' rhyme?

3. The word 'monkey' has 'key' in it. Can you think of two more animals with 'key' in their names?

4. What is the answer to the riddle?

Writing

1. Here are two catch rhymes. Write them down and try them out on friends.

Round and round the rugged rock *The ragged rascal ran.* *Say how many 'r's in that* *And you're a clever man.*

Adam and Eve and Pinch Me *Went down to the river to bathe.* *Adam and Eve were drowned.* *Who do you think was saved?*

2. Copy these 'ant' riddles and match them up with the correct answers.

   What kind of ant is a young child?   **pant**s

   What kind of ant is a very tall man?   **plant**s

   What kind of ants do you wear?   in**fant**

   What kind of ant is a place to eat?   **ant**lers

   What kind of ants grow in the garden?   restau**rant**

   What kind of ants do deer have?   gi**ant**

3. See copymaster 30 for some more riddles to solve.

Three steps to writing poetry

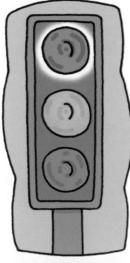

Ready

- Work with someone else if you can.
- Talk about your ideas together.
- Write down your ideas in rough.
- Don't worry too much about spelling or punctuation.

Steady

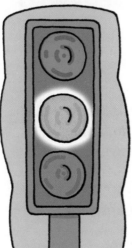

- Read what you have written.
- Talk about your ideas. Can you make them any better?
- Cross out any ideas you don't like.
- Add words you want to or take words out you don't like.
- Improve the words you have used.
- Try to use interesting, powerful or descriptive words.

Write

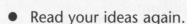

- Read your ideas again.
- Choose the best ideas for your poem.
- Check them for spelling mistakes.
- Check the punctuation.
- Think about the best way of setting out your ideas in your book (or on a computer).
- Make a best copy of your poem.
- Decorate or illustrate it to make it look good if you have time.